An Easter Collection
for Children's Programs

 Abingdon Press

AN EASTER COLLECTION

Copyright © 2000 by Abingdon Press

ISBN 0-687-015081

00 01 02 03 04 05 06 07 08 09 — 10 9 8 7 6 5 4 3 2 1

PRINTED IN THE UNITED STATES OF AMERICA

CONTENTS

NO FLOWERS FOR EASTER
Elaine Clanton Harpine
Production Notes

You may present this play with as few as three children (Jenny, Gary, and Linda) or as many as twenty. Simply combine roles to fit the size of your group.

Play begins in silence. Have children sitting on the floor or standing around a table packing grocery bags of canned food. Children stream in carrying canned goods. Gary snaps open a paper sack, making a loud noise. Jenny enters from off stage as group continues packing bags.

Characters

Jenny
Gary
Linda
other children as desired

JENNY: We'll have to cancel. That's the only thing to do.

GARY: What on earth are you talking about?

JENNY: Easter! We have to cancel Easter.

CHILD: Why?

JENNY: The flowers haven't come. We can't have Easter without flowers.

CHILD: Who cares about flowers? They just stink up the sanctuary anyway.

JENNY: It wouldn't be Easter without flowers. Hyacinths, tulips, daffodils . . .

CHILD: Easter Lilies!

CHILD: Jenny has a point. I've never heard of an Easter service without flowers.

CHILD: Easter's more than flowers.

JENNY: Oh, I know, there's . . .

CHILD: Butterflies!

CHILD: Easter eggs!

CHILD: Fancy hats!

CHILD: A new dress.

CHILD: Shoes that pinch my toes.

CHILD: And ties that choke you to death.

CHILD: Yummy fresh baked bread!

CHILD: Easter grass!

CHILD: The sunrise service *(said with dread in the voice as child pretends to fall down from exhaustion.)*

LINDA: No! No! No! *(with disgust)* Easter's not about flowers and Easter grass. Easter's a celebration of love.

GARY: Is that why we have butterflies and flowers? To remind us of God's love?

JENNY: I thought the butterfly was a symbol of the resurrection?

CHILD: New life!

LINDA: It's both.

CHILD: I know, I know. God loves us so much God sent his Son to show us how to love. God wants us to go out and love others.

CHILD: What others?

LINDA: Everyone!

GARY: Even strangers?

LINDA: You don't go up and hug a stranger, but Jesus did tell us to care even abut people we don't know.

CHILD: Feed the hungry!

CHILD: House the homeless!

CHILD: Save the whales!

JENNY: Will you be serious!

CHILD: We are.

LINDA: Jesus said to feed those who are hungry.

GARY: Give shelter to those who sleep on the street.

JENNY: I can't build a house. I wouldn't know the first thing to do.

LINDA: You don't have to.

CHILD: All you have to do is care.

CHILD: If you really care, you'll find a way to help.

GARY: Remember that box of nails we bought for the Habitat for Humanity house downtown? We didn't actually build the house, but we did help by earning the money to buy a box of nails.

CHILD: Let's buy a window this year.

JENNY: That would cost a lot more money.

LINDA: We can do it.

ALL: Yeah! Let's buy a window.

CHILD: And these food bags we're filling—that's a way of showing we care.

CHILD: We should do more. After all, it is Easter.

CHILD: Instead of just collecting cans of food, we could cook an actual Easter dinner.

CHILD: My mom says that many shut-ins don't get food deliveries on holidays because Meals-on-Wheels can't find enough volunteers to cook and deliver the food.

JENNY: You mean the people don't get anything to eat?

CHILD: Sometimes churches help.

LINDA: We could help

GARY: Finally something besides collecting cans of beans and peas.

CHILD: I know. I hate collecting cans.

JENNY: Cooking a meal would be better. I'd feel more like I actually helped someone.

CHILD: I brought a whole dollar for the Heifer Project collection this morning. I earned it cleaning out the garage. Does that help?

LINDA: It sure does. The dairy goat we're buying to send to the Native American Reservation in El Paso will not only give food to feed their families but a steady job. They can build new homes. Send their children to school.

GARY: I think instead of buying flowers to smell up the sanctuary this year, we should help people in need. We can buy a window, collect food, raise the money for a dairy goat, and cook a big Easter dinner.

JENNY: We could deliver it on Easter day.

LINDA: There's a lady with two children who lives down the street from us. She fell and broke her leg. She's out of work. Can't cook. She really need helps.

JENNY: We have bags and bags of food.

GARY: And we could deliver Easter dinner hot from the church kitchen to their front door.

LINDA: We'd better ask my mom first, but I think she'll say yes.

GARY: What do you say? Everybody want to?

ALL: Yes!

JENNY: Even if we don't have flowers, this could turn out to be the best Easter ever.

SIX WHO PASS ON THEIR WAY TO EASTER

Barbara T. Rowland

Production Notes

Max (or Maxine) sits on stool center stage. Holds ball and tosses it from hand to hand. Players enter stage right and exit stage left. The three adults may be played by children.

Props

Grocery bag with carton of eggs
Shopping bag with dress
fishing poles
Rabbit *(live or stuffed - if stuffed it should look realistic)*
small pieces of lumber and hammer
picnic basket(s)
backpack(s)

Characters

Children	**Max**	**Claire**
	Brad	**Gus**
	Elsie	**Dan**
	Luke	**Maggie**
	Lauren	**Bill**
Adults	**Mr. Alexander**	
	Mrs. Alexander	
	Granddad	

MAX: My Mom said to wait here for Granddad. She went to work and Dad's out-of-town somewhere. Granddad's goin' to help me get ready for Easter. What do we do to get ready for Easter? *(Shrugs)* Guess I'll find out. Mom and I never did anything about it. *(Hears whistling and looks stage right as Brad enters carrying a grocery bag.)* Hey Brad, whatcha got?

BRAD: It's my Easter egg stuff! Mom let me go to the corner store and get what we need to get ready for Easter! See?

9

	(Pulls out carton of eggs) We're going to dye eggs to hide and hunt.
MAX:	So that's how you get ready for Easter! Maybe my granddad and I will do that. He's coming to get me so we can get ready for Easter. Sound like fun!
BRAD:	It is! After we dye the eggs, I write on 'em and stick stickers on 'em. We take turns hiding them and hunting them. It's a lotta fun. Gotta go get started. See ya.
MAX:	See ya. Have a happy Easter. I guess that's what you do to get ready for Easter. Maybe someone else will come along to play with me while I wait.
ELSIE:	*(Hurries onto playing area carrying shopping bag from clothing store.)* Hi, Max.
MAX:	Hi, Elsie. Wanna play catch awhile?
ELSIE:	Oh, no. I'm going to show Sue my new Easter dress. Wanna see?
MAX:	Well, okay, I guess.
ELSIE:	*(Takes dress and hat from bag and hold it up.)* See? It's my beautiful new Easter dress and hat! I can't wait to wear them to church Easter Sunday!
MAX:	Is that how you get ready for Easter? Get new clothes?
ELSIE:	Well, I guess that's important. Mother and I always go shopping before Easter. Aren't you going to get new clothes?
MAX:	I don't know. My granddad is coming to help me get ready for Easter.
ELSIE:	Oh. Well, he'll probably take you shopping. Bye. I'm going on to Sue's house.
MAX:	Bye, Elsie. Hmmm. Clothes and eggs. Wonder which Granddad will choose for Easter. *(Hears arguing and looks*

right. Luke and Lauren should ad lib an argument about who will carry the bait.) Hey, Luke and Lauren! What's going on?

LUKE: Daddy is taking us fishing on Easter and we got some bait at the store!

LAUREN: And I want to carry it!

LUKE: So do I! We've never gone for bait by ourselves before and I am the oldest!

LAUREN: Not by much, you're not! I can carry it as well as you can!

MAX: *(stands)* Let me see. *(looks in box)* Ugh, creepy crawlers. Glad I don't have to hold them. One might get out and crawl up my arm!

LAUREN: I never thought of that. Here, Luke, you carry the worms.

LUKE: O. K. But we better get home. Dad may be ready to go since he's off work today.

LAUREN: Let's go. Bye Max. What are you doing for Easter?

MAX: I don't know yet. My granddad is coming.

LUKE: See ye. Bye.

(Luke and Lauren exit. Max sits.)

MAX: Wish somebody would play with me while I wait. Everybody has somethin' to do but me. *(glances right)* What's coming?

(Enter three children. One carries a rabbit. Others hold lumber and a hammer.

MAX: Hey! What's going on?

CLAIRE: Look at my bunny! Dad gave it to me for Easter!

GUS: We're going to help her build a cage for it.

DAN: Yeah. Her mother said it couldn't come in the house.

MAX: You got a rabbit for Easter?

11

CLAIRE:	Yes. Surely you've heard of the Easter Bunny? Well, this is MY Easter bunny!
GUS:	Let's go. I want to get started.
DAN:	Yeah. I never built a rabbit cage.
MAX:	Well, good luck! And happy Easter, I guess.
CLAIRE, GUS, AND DAN:	Bye! Hope the Easter Bunny finds you! *(exit)*
MAX:	Wonder what the Easter Bunny would do if he found me? Wonder what Granddad will do to get ready for Easter? Wish he would get here. Hey, the Alexanders are putting stuff in their car. *(calls to them)* Hi! Goin' somewhere?

Family enters carrying baskets of food and backpacks.

MRS. ALEXANDER:	Hi, Max. Yes. We're going to a family picnic.
MR. ALEXANDER:	We all get together for Easter at the State Park.
MAGGIE:	It's lots of fun playing with my cousins!
BILL:	And we have tons of good food! Fried chicken, chocolate cake; that's the best part.
MRS. ALEXANDER:	What are you doing for Easter, Max?
MAX:	I don't know. My granddad's coming.
MR. ALEXANDER:	Well, that's good. Have a happy Easter. *(to family)* Now let's get on our way.
MAGGIE AND BILL:	Bye, Max! See ya after Easter!
MAX:	Bye. Have fun. *(sits)* Well, let's see, seems that people *(counts on fingers)* dye Easter eggs, buy new clothes, go fishing, get—or give—rabbits, eat a lot and visit family at Easter. Which will Granddad choose? Wonder when he'll get here?
GRANDDAD:	*(Enters stage right.)* Hi there, Max!

MAX:	*(Jumps up)* Granddad! I thought you'd never get here!
GRANDDAD:	Well, here I am and we have lots to do.
MAX:	What? Mom said you'd help me get ready for Easter. But what will we do? People passed while I was waiting. They're doing different things about Easter.
GRANDDAD:	That's right. But we know Easter is our celebration of Jesus' rising from the dead after he was crucified. And because he lives, we can be forgiven for our bad choices and live with God in heaven after we die.
MAX:	But how do we celebrate? Have a party?
GRANDDAD:	Not exactly. We'll praise God and thank God at church and at home. And we'll do other things, too.

(As he continues, the five groups enter stage left, pass behind Max and Granddad and form a semi-circle so that all may be seen.)

We'll dye eggs pretty colors and hide and hunt them. New life hatches from eggs, so eggs are a symbol of Easter.

We'll wear new spring clothes to show that we have new life through Jesus.

We'll "fish" for souls rather than swimming fish. We do that by telling others the good news of Jesus' payment for our wrong-doing. And we invite others to worship with us.

We may give or receive gifts to show love and thankfulness for God's great gift to us.

We'll worship and feast with family and friends as we celebrate the resurrection of Jesus!

MAX:	All right! Granddad! Let's get ready for Easter.

Suggested closings:
   1. Say a prayer that our celebration of Easter will be pleasing to God.
   2. Actors may sing an Easter song or hymn.
   3. Actors may be joined by children's choir for Easter music.

EASTER ACROSTICS

Children hold the letters that spell E-A–S-T-E-R and/or J-O-Y. If you have older children they can speak the lines that go with their letters; for younger children have an older child or adult read the lines as children step forward.

E   E is for early. The women came to the tomb early in the morning.

A   A is for the angel who rolled away the stone.

S   S is for sorrow. Jesus' friends were sad.

T   T is for the tears they cried.

E   E is for excitement. The angel told the women, "Jesus is not here!"

R   R is for "Risen as he said."

ALL: Happy Easter!

J   J is for Jesus.

O   O is for God's only Son.

Y   Y is for you! Jesus came for you!

ALL: Happy Easter! Jesus lives!

EASTER EGGS

For seven children. Prepare seven large plastic Easter eggs as follows:
1. *Put in a piece of cloth and a bit of palm branch.*
2. *Put in a piece of broken bread.*
3. *Put in a thorn.*
4. *Put in a small cross*
5. *Put in a small flat stone*
6. *Put in a cinnamon stick and cloves*
7. *Leave this egg empty.*

Children stand in a line, then step forward, one by one to open their eggs and speak their lines.

CHILD 1: My egg holds a piece of cloth and a bit of palm branch. These symbols remind us that people greeted Jesus with palm leaves and threw their coats on the road.

CHILD 2: My egg holds a piece of broken bread to remind us of the Last Supper.

CHILD 3: My egg holds a thorn to remind us that Jesus wore a crown of thorns.

CHILD 4: My egg holds a cross to remind us that Jesus gave his life for us.

Child 5: My egg holds a stone to remind us of the tomb where Jesus was buried.

Child 6: My egg holds spices to remind us of the spices the women took to the tomb.

Child 7: My egg is empty, just like the the tomb on that wonderful morning.

ALL: Jesus is alive!

THANK YOU, GOD, FOR EASTER
A FINGERPLAY

by Linda R. Whited

Five happy children came to church on Easter Day.
(Wiggle all five fingers.)

The first child said, "Thank you, God, for Easter.
It's such a happy day."
(Hold up one finger.)

The second child said, "Thank you, God, for Sunday school,
where we can learn and pray."
(Hold up two fingers.)

The third child said, "Thank you, God, for music
and the songs we love to sing."
(Hold up three fingers.)

The fourth child said, "Thank you, God, for butterflies;
and thank you, God, for spring."
(Hold up four fingers.)

The fifth child said, "Thank you, God, for Jesus,
who came new life to bring."
(Hold up five fingers.)

Five happy children came to church on Easter Day to
thank God for Jesus and for time to learn and pray.
(Wiggle all five fingers.)

BLESSED IS THE ONE

LEADER: Jesus healed the leapers and those who were blind.

CHILDREN: Blessed is the one who comes in the name of the Lord!

LEADER: Jesus fed the hungry.

CHILDREN: Blessed is the one who comes in the name of the Lord!

LEADER: Jesus taught about God's love.

CHILDREN: Blessed is the one who comes in the name of the Lord!

LEADER: People praised the Son of God.

CHILDREN: Blessed is the one who comes in the name of the Lord!

LEADER: Children sang praises to Jesus.

CHILDREN: Blessed is the one who comes in the name of the Lord!

LEADER: We, too, praise God for Jesus, the Savior.

CHILDREN: Blessed is the one who comes in the name of the Lord!

LEADER: Hosanna! Praise be to God!

CHILDREN: Blessed is the one who comes in the name of the Lord!

PRAYING IN THE GARDEN

by Rebecca J. Kerr

You may wish to use the following three reader's theatre pieces during Sunday morning worship services, mid-week services, or as a devotional time before Sunday school. Use as many or as few people as you wish.

READER 1: After eating the Passover meal, Jesus and eleven of his disciples sang a hymn. Judas had already left the upper room alone. Then Jesus and the disciples went out to the Mount of Olives.

ALL: Going to the garden to pray for strength and guidance.

READER 2: On the way, Jesus said to the disciples, "You will all desert me tonight." "Not I," said Peter. "I will never leave you." "Yes, Peter, on this very night, before the cock crows, you will deny me three times."

ALL: Going to the garden to pray for strength and guidance.

READER 2: When they reached the Mount of Olives, Jesus and the disciples went into the garden of Gethsemane. The word *gethsemane* means olive press. The garden was called Gethsemane because people pressed the oil from olives that grew on olive trees in the garden.

ALL: Going to the garden to pray for strength and guidance.

READER 4: Jesus said to the disciples, "I want to go and pray. Peter, James, and John, come with me. The rest of you sit here and wait for me." Peter, James, and John followed Jesus into the garden. He said to them, "I feel great sorrow. I want to go farther into the garden alone. Stay here and stay awake with me."

ALL: All are in the garden to pray for strength and guidance.

READER 5: Jesus went farther into the garden, where he fell to the ground and prayed: "My Father, I do not want to suffer and die; I want to live. If it is possible, remove this cup of suffering from me; yet not what I want, but what you want be done."

ALL: Praying in the garden, praying for strength and guidance.

READER 6: Jesus then returned to Peter, James, and John and found them sleeping. Jesus awakened Peter and said, "Peter, could you not stay awake with me for one hour? Stay awake now and pray."

ALL: Praying in the garden, praying for strength and guidance.

READER 7: Jesus went away a second time. This time he prayed: "My Father, if what you want cannot happen unless I drink this cup of suffering, I accept it. Your will be done."

ALL: Praying in the garden, praying for strength and guidance.

READER 8: Jesus returned and found the disciples sleeping. Jesus said to the disciples, "Are you still sleeping and resting? Get up and let's go! The time has come for me to be betrayed. Don't you hear that noise?"

ALL: Should we leave the garden, where he prayed for strength and guidance?

READER 9: A great crowd of people carrying swords and clubs came into the garden. The disciple Judas was with them. He walked up to Jesus and kissed him, saying, "Greetings, Rabbi!"

ALL: Should we leave the garden where he prayed for strength and guidance?

READER 10: Then the crowd seized Jesus. Judas had told the chief priests that the man he would kiss would be Jesus. Jesus asked, "Have you come out with swords and clubs to arrest me as though I were a bandit? Day after day I sat in the Temple teaching, and you did not arrest me."

ALL: Should we leave the garden where he prayed for strength and guidance?

READER 11: The disciples were all afraid that the crowd would seize them too. They fled, leaving Jesus alone with his captors.

ALL: Yes, we will leave the garden, where he prayed for strength and guidance.

READER 12: The crowd then led Jesus away to be tried and condemned.

ALL: He prayed in the garden; he prayed for strength and guidance.

(Based on Matthew 26:30-50, 55-56)

THE ROOSTER CROWED

by Rebecca J. Kerr

NARRATOR: When Jesus was arrested, Peter followed the crowd to the house of the high priest, Caiaphas. The members of the Sanhedrin, the Jewish religious court, were trying Jesus to find evidence so they could sentence him to death. Peter waited in the courtyard with other people to see what would happen. The night was chilly, so someone started a small fire in the middle of the courtyard. The crowd moved toward the fire, and Peter joined them.

SERVANT GIRL 1: *(to Peter)* I know you. I have seen you before. You were with Jesus.

PETER: I do not know what you are talking about.
(He turns to hide his face.)

NARRATOR: Peter went to the porch. A little later another servant girl saw him.

SERVANT GIRL 2:   *(turning to bystanders and pointing to Peter)* This man was with Jesus.

PETER: I do not know the man!

NARRATOR: After a little while a bystander recognized Peter and came up to him.

BYSTANDER: You must know Jesus; your voice sounds like that of a Galilean.

PETER: I tell you, I do not know this man!

NARRATOR: At that moment the cock crowed. Then Peter remembered what Jesus had said: "Before the cock crows, you will deny me three time." Peter left the courtyard. He was so sad that he began to weep bitterly.

(Based on Matthew 26:58, 69-75)

NARRATOR: The morning after Jesus was arrested, the crowd bound him and took him to Pilate, the Roman governor of the region. The Romans ruled the country at that time, and only the Romans could put a person to death.

COUNCIL MEMBER: We wish to have this man crucified.

PILATE: Why? What crime has he done?

COUNCIL MEMBER: He is causing trouble. He is telling people that he is the king of the Jews.

PILATE: *(to Jesus)* Are you the King of the Jews?

JESUS: You have said so.

PILATE: Don't you hear how many things they are saying against you?

NARRATOR: Jesus gave no answer, but stood quietly.

PILATE: This man is amazing!

NARRATOR: Each year during Passover, the Roman governor set free one criminal that the crowd wanted. Pilate knew that he had one bad prisoner named Barabbas.

PILATE: I cannot find anything wrong with this man. I can release one prisoner for you. Do you want me to let Jesus go?

CROWD: No! Jesus is claiming to have the rights and qualities of God. He is trying to destroy the laws of Moses.

PILATE: Do you want me to release Barabbas or Jesus?

CROWD: Release Barabbas!

PILATE: Then what should I do with Jesus?

CROWD: Crucify him!

PILATE: Why? What evil has he done? He has not committed a crime.

CROWD: Crucify him!

NARRATOR: Pilate was afraid that a riot was beginning. He took some water and washed his hands in front of the crowd.

PILATE: I wash my hands of this. I am innocent of this man's blood.

NARRATOR: Pilate then released Barabbas, and the soldiers led Jesus away. They took Jesus to the hill called Golgotha, which means *Place of a Skull*, where he was crucified.

(Based on Matthew 27:1-2, 11-54.)

WHAT HAPPENED AT THE TOMB?

by Rebecca J. Kerr

Characters

Reporter
Joseph of Arimathea
Mary Magdalene
Mary

(Someone holds up a sign reading, SATURDAY)

REPORTER: Good evening. This is Jerusalem's roving reporter, Simon David. As you know, a tragedy occurred in our city yesterday. Jesus of Nazareth, whom some say was the Messiah, was put to death on a cross. I'm here in the garden of a man named Joseph of Arimathea. Joseph, tell us what happened after Jesus died.

JOSEPH OF ARIMATHEA: I went to Pilate, the Roman governor, and asked for Jesus' body. And Pilate gave it to me.

REPORTER: What did you do with the body?

JOSEPH OF ARIMATHEA: I first wrapped the body in clean linen cloth. Then I laid it in my own new tomb, which I had carved out of the rock here in my garden. I rolled a great stone over the door of the tomb.

REPORTER: I see some soldiers outside the tomb. Why are they there?

JOSEPH OF ARIMATHEA: The chief priests asked Pilate to have some soldiers stand guard outside the tomb.

REPORTER: Why?

JOSEPH OF ARIMATHEA: They were afraid that the disciples would steal the body and claim that Jesus had been raised from the dead. You know that Jesus said before his death that he would rise again. The soldiers were ordered to guard the tomb until the third day.

REPORTER: Did anyone else know where Jesus was buried?

JOSEPH OF ARIMATHEA: Yes. Two women named Mary—one was Mary Magdalene—were here when we buried him.

REPORTER: *(turning to the audience and saying in a sad, quiet voice)* This report closes this sad, sad, story. Good night.

(Someone holds up a sign reading, SUNDAY)

REPORTER: *(speaking to the audience)* Good morning! This is Jerusalem's roving reporter, Simon David, here again near the tomb of Jesus in Joseph of Arimathea's garden. This time I have with me the two women, Mary and Mary Magdalene, who were here when Jesus was buried. *(turning to Mary Magdalene)* When did you come to the tomb?

MARY MAGDALENE: We came to the tomb after the sabbath, at dawn.

REPORTER: *(to Mary)* What happened while you were walking to the tomb?

MARY. Suddenly the earth began to shake.

REPORTER: What did the soldiers do?

MARY MAGDALENE: They were so afraid they were shaking.

REPORTER: Weren't you afraid?

MARY MAGDALENE: I was afraid too, but I also felt that something wonderful had happened.

23

REPORTER:	How did you know that something wonderful had happened?
MARY:	An angel told us what had happened!
REPORTER:	An angel! Where did you see an angel?
MARY:	The angel was sitting on the stone that had been blocking the entrance to the tomb. Now we could see right into the tomb.
REPORTER:	What did the angel say?
MARY MAGDALENE:	The angel said: "Do not be afraid. I know that you are looking for Jesus. He is not here; for he has been raised, as he said. Come, see the place where he lay. Then go quickly and tell the disciples that Jesus lives."
REPORTER:	That is good news. How did you feel about what the angel said?
MARY:	My joy was so great that I wanted to shout!
REPORTER:	What did you do?
MARY MAGDALENE:	We ran to find the disciples, but . . .
REPORTER:	But what?
MARY MAGDALENE:	But, on the way Jesus appeared to us!
REPORTER:	That had to surprise you!
MARY:	It did, but Jesus spoke to us. He said, "Do not be afraid; go and tell the others."
REPORTER:	*(turning to the audience)* Well, now you have heard the good news. Jesus is risen! Jesus lives.

(Based on Matthew 27:55-66; 28: 1-10)

LENTEN WORSHIP READINGS

by Rebecca J. Kerr

Use these readings in your classroom or as part of the worship service. An easy way to make a Lenten cross is to use newpapers. You will need about 40 full sheets of newspaper; foil; a paring knife; masking tape; 6 purple candles and 1 white candle. Follow these directions.

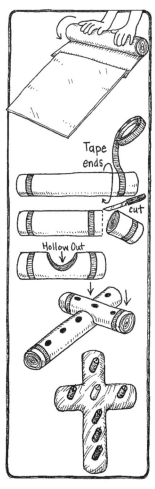

1. Tightly roll one sheet of newspaper; then lay the end of the next sheet over the end of the first sheet and continue rolling. Continue adding a sheet of newspaper to the end of the previously rolled sheet until it is the size of a log. (You will need about 20 full sheets of newspaper per log.)

2. Wrap masking tape around the log to keep it from unrolling. then make another log.

3. Cut off about one-third of the end of one of the logs to make it shorter than the other. On the back of the shorter log, hollow out a section in the center. This will enable the two logs to fit together to form a cross (see picture).

4. Put the logs together to determine where to put the holes for the candles (see picture for the placement of holes). Using the paring knife, hollow out seven holes on the top of the cross. Then take the logs apart again.

5. Completely cover the newspaper logs with foil.

6. Push the foil down into the hollow on the shorter log. Use a pencil to poke through the foil at the holes.

7. Wrap a small piece of foil around the bottom of each candle and then put the candle in a hole. Put the white candle in the hole in the cross where the two logs intersect.

First Sunday in Lent

READER 1: The Lenten cross is the like the Advent wreath. We use the Advent wreath to help us prepare to celebrate Christmas. Each week during Advent we light candles on the Advent wreath to remember Jesus' birth.

READER 2: We use a Lenten cross to help us prepare to celebrate Easter. Each week during Lent we light a purple candle on the Lenten cross to remember Jesus. We use a cross to hold our candles because the cross is a symbol for Easter and Lent.

READER 3: Lent is a journey toward Easter. It is a time to remember Jesus—his life, his words, and his actions.

READER 4: Today is the first Sunday of Lent, so we will light the first candle on our cross.

READER 5: The first candle reminds us of Jesus the teacher. Jesus taught us to love God and one another. *(Light the first purple candle.)*

ALL: *(Sing "Tell Me the Stories of Jesus.")*

ALL: We praise God who sent Jesus to teach us the way to live.

Second Sunday in Lent

READER 1: Today is the second Sunday in Lent, so we will light two candles on our Lenten cross.

READER 2: The first candle reminds us of Jesus the teacher. Jesus taught us to love God and one another.
(Light the first purple candle.)

READER 3: Today we light the second candle to remind us of Jesus the healer. *(Light the second purple candle.)*

READER 4: Jesus loves and has compassion for everyone.

ALL: *(Sing "Jesus' Hands Were Kind Hands," or a familiar song.)*

ALL: We can show love and compassion for others who are sick or have disabilities.

READER 5: Jesus gave people new life.

ALL: We can give new life by loving and caring for others.

ALL: *(say aloud in unison)*

> I will sing to the Lord
>   as long as I live;
> I will sing praise to my God
>   while I have being.

Psalm 104:33 NRSV

Third Sunday in Lent

READER 1: Today is the third Sunday in Lent, so we will light three purple candles on our Lenten cross.

READER 2: The first candle reminds us of Jesus the teacher. Jesus taught us to love God and one another.
(Light the first purple candle.)

READER 3: The second candle reminds us of Jesus the healer.
(Light the second purple candle.)

READER 4: Today we light the third candle to remind us of Jesus in God's house. *(Light the third purple candle.)*

READER 5: Jesus showed us that God's house should be a place of prayer, praise, and healing.

READER 6: Our church is God's house.

READER 7: Our church is a special place where we can worship and praise God. We can say and sing our praises to God and Jesus in our church.

ALL: *(say aloud in unison)*

> I will sing to the Lord
>   as long as I live;
> I will sing praise to my God
>   while I have being.

Psalm 104:33 NRSV

READER 8: Our church is a place of prayer, a place where we can pray for others and for ourselves.

READER 9: Our church is a place to help others, as Jesus taught us to do.

ALL: (*pray aloud in unison*) Thank you, God, for our church.

Fourth Sunday in Lent

READER 1: Today is the fourth Sunday in Lent, so we will light four purple candles on our Lenten Cross.

READER 2: The first candle reminds us of Jesus the teacher. Jesus taught us to love God and one another.
(Light the first purple candle.)

READER 3: The second candle reminds us of Jesus the healer.
(Light the second purple candle.)

READER 4: The third candle reminds us of Jesus in God's house.
(Light the third purple candle.)

READER 5: Today we light the fourth candle to remind us of the Last Supper Jesus had with his disciples.
(Light the fourth purple candle.)

READER 6: At the Last Supper Jesus gave his disciples and us a special way to remember him.

READER 7: When we take the bread and cup during Holy Communion, we remember Jesus; what he said and what he did.

READER 8: Jesus loved and had compassion for everyone. He healed many who were sick.

ALL: We remember, we remember.

READER 9: The people loved Jesus. When he rode into Jerusalem, they waved leafy branches and shouted, "Hosanna!"

ALL: We remember, we remember.

READER 10: During the Last Supper Jesus ate with his disciples, he took the bread, blessed it, and broke it. "Take, eat; this is my body," he told his disciples.

ALL: We remember, we remember.

READER 11: Jesus held up the cup and gave thanks. "Drink from it, for this is my blood," he told his disciples.

ALL: We remember, we remember.

READER 12: We eat bread and drink grape juice in Holy Communion.

ALL: *(pray aloud in unison)* And we remember; we remember Jesus. Thank you, God, for Jesus. Amen.

Fifth Sunday in Lent

READER 1: Today is the fifth Sunday in Lent, so we will light five purple candles on our Lenten cross.

READER 2: The first candle reminds us of Jesus the teacher. Jesus taught us to love God and one another.
(Light the first purple candle.)

READER 3: The second candle reminds us of Jesus the healer.
(Light the second purple candle.)

READER 4: The third candle reminds of Jesus in God's house.
(Light the third purple candle.)

READER 5: The fourth candle reminds us of the Last Supper Jesus held with his disciples. *(Light the fourth purple candle.)*

READER 6: Today we light the fifth candle to remind us of Jesus praying in the garden. *(Light the fifth purple candle.)*

READER 7: Jesus prayed to God often.

ALL: We can pray to God too.

READER 8: Jesus and the disciples went to the garden to pray.

ALL: We can pray in our gardens, yards, homes, anywhere.

READER 9: It was a difficult time for Jesus.

ALL: We face difficult times and have to make difficult decisions.

READER 10: Jesus prayed for strength and guidance.

ALL: We can pray for strength and guidance too.

ALL: *(pray aloud in unison)* Thank you, God, for listening to our prayers. Thank you for your help in difficult times. Amen.

Sixth Sunday in Lent

READER 1: Today is the sixth Sunday in Lent, so we will light six purple candles on our Lenten cross.

READER 2: The first candle reminds us of Jesus the teacher. Jesus taught us to love God and one another.
(Light the first purple candle.)

READER 3: The second candle reminds us of Jesus the healer.
(Light the second purple candle.)

READER 4: The third candle reminds of of Jesus in God's house.
(Light the third purple candle.)

READER 5: The fourth candle reminds us of the Last Supper Jesus had with his disciples. *(Light the fourth purple candle.)*

READER 6: The fifth candle reminds us of Jesus praying in the garden. *(Light the fifth purple candle.)*

READER 7: Today we light the sixth candle to remind us of Peter's sorrow for denying Jesus. *(Light the sixth purple candle.)*

READER 8: Jesus said to Peter, "Before the cock crows, you will deny me three times."

ALL: Peter answered, "Even though I must die with you, I will not deny you."

READER 9: Peter waited in the courtyard as Jesus was being tried.

ALL: I am so afraid, Lord.

READER 10: Three times Peter denied even knowing Jesus.

ALL: Then Peter heard the cock crow, and he wept.

READER 11: Peter wept because he was sorry he had denied knowing Jesus.

ALL: And God forgave Peter.

READER 12: We can be sorry for our mistakes too.

ALL: And God will forgive us.

Easter Sunday

READER 1: Today the Lenten cross becomes an Easter cross.

READER 2: Today we light the white candle, the Easter candle, to remind us that Jesus lives. *(Light the white candle.)*

READER 3: He is not here; for he has been raised, as he said. *(Matthew 28:6a)*

ALL: He has been raised indeed! Praise be to God! Hallelujah!

READER 4: He has been raised for you and for me.

ALL: Jesus lives! Praise be to God!

READER 5: It is like a butterfly springing to life and leaving behind an empty cocoon.

ALL: Jesus lives! Praise be to God!

READER 6: Everything is beautiful and alive. Jesus gives new life.

READER 7: Easter is a time of joy. We can share our joy of Easter with others.

ALL: Jesus lives! Praise be to God!

READER 8: We can tell others about Jesus.

ALL: Praise be to God for Jesus and for new life!

ALL: *(Sing an Easter song.)*

EASTER THANKS

by Nancy Ashley Young

O give thanks (clap, clap)
  to the Lord our God;
He is good. (clap, clap)
He is good indeed!
O give thanks (clap, clap)
  for his steadfast love;
It endures (clap, clap)
  forever, (clap, clap)
  for good, (clap, clap)
  Indeed! (clap, clap, clap, clap)
The Lord has risen. (clap, clap)
The Lord has risen indeed!
The Lord has risen. (clap, clap)
The Lord has risen indeed!
The Lord has risen. (clap, clap)
The Lord has risen indeed!
O give thanks (clap, clap)
  to the Lord! (clap, clap)
Indeed! (clap, clap, clap, clap)

(Based on Psalm 118:1; Luke 24:34.)